To Richard,
Have a great 2008!

The Sailors

Birth of a Navy

by Edward W. Lull

Copyright © 2007 by Edward W. Lull

All rights reserved. No part of this book shall be reproduced or transmitted in any form or by any means, electronic, mechanical, magnetic, photographic including photocopying, recording or by any information storage and retrieval system, without prior written permission of the publisher. No patent liability is assumed with respect to the use of the information contained herein. Although every precaution has been taken in the preparation of this book, the publisher and author assume no responsibility for errors or omissions. Neither is any liability assumed for damages resulting from the use of the information contained herein.

ISBN 0-7414-4323-6

Illustrations courtesy of The Mariners' Museum, Norfolk, VA

Published by:

INFI∞ITY
PUBLISHING.COM

1094 New DeHaven Street, Suite 100
West Conshohocken, PA 19428-2713
Info@buybooksontheweb.com
www.buybooksontheweb.com
Toll-free (877) BUY BOOK
Local Phone (610) 941-9999
Fax (610) 941-9959

Printed in the United States of America
Printed on Recycled Paper
Published October 2007

Acknowledgments

Illustrations provided by: **The Mariners' Museum Newport News, VA**

The author expresses his appreciation to the following individuals who assisted in the book's development:

Claudia A. Jew
Director, Photographic Services
Licensing and Publications
The Mariners' Museum

Sigrid Trumpy
Curator,
The Beverley R. Robinson Collection
U.S. Naval Academy Museum

James Cheever
Senior Curator
U.S. Naval Academy Museum

Dedication

This book is about some of the heroic men whose daring and courageous deeds in the early days of the United States Navy left a permanent legacy for those who followed. We live in a different age with a navy of quite a different sort from the sailing ships of the early days of our nation. However, the basic characteristics of the men the reader will meet in this book represent the formula for success in fighting men of any age.

There was no Naval Academy then; midshipmen learned their trade at sea. Today's midshipmen must undergo extensive training and education to be properly prepared to accept the proud title of Ensign, United States Navy. This book is dedicated to you:

Midshipmen, U.S. Navy.

Which of you will be the next Stephen Decatur, Thomas Macdonough, Oliver Hazard Perry, ...etc.

Table of Contents

Title	Page
Acknowledgments	i
Dedication	ii
Prologue	v
1. "Saucy Jack" Barry	1
2. The Battle off Flamborough Head	11
3. Burning of *Philadelphia*	19
4. The Attack on Tripoli	31
5. The Birth of Old Ironsides	39
6. *Macedonian* Meets *United States*	47
7. *Constitution* Versus *Java*	55
8. "Don't Give Up the Ship..."	61
9. The Battle of Lake Erie	69
10. The Final Cruise of *Essex*	77
11. The Battle of Lake Champlain	87
12. The End of Barbary Piracy	99
Epilogue	109
The Author	111

List of Illustrations

Title		Page
1-1	Portrait of Commodore John Barry	2
1-2	Capture of HMS Edward	4
1-3	Alliance vs. Atalanta and Trepassy	7
2-1	Portrait of John Paul Jones	12
2-2	Bonhomme Richard vs. HMS Serapis	16
3-1	The Burning of *Philadelphia*	27
4-1	Attack on Tripoli	34
4-2	Stephen Decatur in Combat	37
5-1	Portrait of Isaac Hull	40
5-2	USS Constitution vs. HMS Guerriere	43
6-1	Portrait of Stephen Decatur	48
6-2	USS United States vs. HMS Macedonian	52
7-1	Portrait of William Bainbridge	56
7-2	USS *Constitution* vs. HMS *Java*	59
8-1	Portrait of James Lawrence	62
8-2	USS *Chesapeake* vs. HMS *Shannon*	67
9-1	Portrait of Oliver Hazard Perry	70
9-2	The Battle of Lake Erie	74
10-1	USS *Essex* Facing HMS *Phoebe* and HMS *Cherub*	83
11-1	Portrait of Thomas Macdonough	88
11-2	Victory at Lake Champlain	93
12-1	USS Guerriere vs. Mashouda	103
12-2	Decatur's Fleet at Algiers	105

Prologue

The submarine seems to hug the water as it slides down the channel on its way toward the open sea to begin deployment. The deck is lined with sailors, standing ceremoniously in ranks wearing their white uniforms, defining the ship as a military man-of-war, honoring its Navy traditions. How vast are these traditions – even to the proud use of the term *sailor* – for the crew members of a nuclear-powered submarine? Loosely defined as "one who sails," the Navy's origin and early history affixed a much deeper meaning to the term than that. In those early days, sailors embraced an unspoken code of courage, commitment, and selflessness as they faced death regularly from battle and the elements. The hardships of life at sea in the cramped sailing ships are just footnotes to the major events historians relate – but they were real and harsh. However, these sailors set a proud and challenging course for others to follow. Their leaders, such as Barry, Jones, Decatur, Perry, Preble, Hull, MacDonough, and others were warriors, in the truest sense of the word.

This book uses the concise and efficient language of poetry to retell stories of actual events that built Navy traditions and made the term *sailor* one of pride, used by the newest "boot" to the Chief of Naval Operations. All events recounted are not successes – but most are; bravery and love of country are evident throughout. The events selected for inclusion in this book are presented in chronological order, from Captain John Barry's exploits in 1776 to Stephen Decatur's exacting peace terms from the Barbary States in 1815.

Return now to that historic period when the fledgling nation attempts to define itself to the world as an independent state – to be dominated by no other. Join the men at sea whose adventures built the traditions that made the United States Navy a symbol for greatness.

1. "Saucy Jack" Barry

One of the early captains in the Navy, John Barry was given command of *Lexington* in 1776. This poem recounts his two most notable wartime encounters: the first while commanding *Lexington*; the second in 1781, while commanding *Alliance*.

1-1. Portrait of Commodore John Barry

"Saucy Jack" Barry

John Barry was born in the County Wexford on the southeast coast of Ireland. In his early life at sea he had earned master's papers prior to arriving in Philadelphia in 1760 at age 25. He became a merchant trader, primarily dealing with the West Indies, as the Colonies moved closer to war with England. In 1775, when he learned that Congress was considering starting a navy, he petitioned to be given a command. An imposing figure at six feet four and powerfully built, he made his case. Barry was given command of *Lexington*, a brig, 84 feet in length. After fitting out, Barry, seventh on the captain's list, took his ship to sea. The year was 1776.

"Sail ho!" the lookout called. "What do you make
it out to be?" The captain hollered back.
"A topsail sloop, inbound," the sailor said.
To close the ship, the captain set his track.

A brilliant sun, an offshore breeze, a day
to be at sea – but soon the placid scene
would be disturbed by battle sounds, and fright
that few had known, and none would call routine.

For Captain Barry, this is what he sought:
the chance to test himself, his ship, his crew.
He ordered, "Beat to quarters!" and the drum
sent sailors to the jobs they'd trained to do.

As ships grew closer, Captain Barry raised
his flag, with thirteen stripes of red and white,
and crosses of St. Andrew and St. George.
Now *Lexington* was ready for a fight.

When just three hundred yards apart, the sloop
unfurled the British Union Jack atop
its mast. A broadside from the sloop began
a battle where the shooting wouldn't stop

1-2. Capture of HMS Edward

until one side surrendered or was sunk.
Although well-trained, the bulk of Barry's men
had never faced a challenge such as this,
where death could strike – but never knowing when.

HMS Edward was the British ship;
its broadside battered *Lexington* astern.
The seven starboard guns of Barry's ship
responded with a salvo in return.

The acrid smoke blew back across the deck,
preventing gunners from reloading fast.
When smoke cleared, they could see their first broadside
had blown away some sails from *Edward*'s mast.

Intensity increased, the battle raged
for two long hours, Barry standing tall
beside the helm; his calm engendered trust.
His crew drew strength and courage through it all.

When *Edward* could no longer carry on,
reluctantly it struck the Union Jack.
The prize crew went aboard with clear commands:
"Keep it afloat, I want to take it back."

Enough repairs were made to take the ship
into Egg Harbor on New Jersey's shore.
This was the first commissioned navy ship
to capture any British man-of-war.

The victory brought fame to Captain John Barry, and led to many other commands and exploits during the Revolutionary War. With the fledgling American Navy significantly outnumbered in ships, men, and guns, many experiences did not result in victories. In fact, confrontations were avoided whenever it appeared that a battle would involve multiple British ships against one Continental ship. However, in 1780, "Saucy Jack" Barry (a nickname he acquired through

his quick wit) was given command of *Alliance*, considered
the Navy's best ship. In 1781 he fought a battle he tried to
avoid.

A convoy job was not what Barry wished,
but its importance he would not dispute.
A French ship laden with food stuffs for troops
could not risk capture while it was en route.

The ocean crossing was a nasty one
including gales that tossed his ship about.
A bolt of lightening split the main topmast
and sails were ripped when hit by waterspout.

One afternoon, a lookout hailed the deck.
"Two sail," he shouted, "off the weather bow."
To get a look, the Captain went aloft:
two sloops-of-war – decision time was now!

He increased sail and turned his ship away,
a two-on-one encounter to avoid.
His job: protect the French ship with the food;
a task he'd fail if his ship were destroyed.

The chase continued on throughout the night;
when dawn broke, Barry saw the sloops had gained.
They hoisted Union Jacks and beat their drums;
to fight – the only option that remained.

Alliance hoisted colors and turned toward;
when close: "What ships are these?" called Saucy Jack.
"His Majesty's sloops *Atalanta* and
Trepassey." Barry quickly hollered back:

"I must advise you, haul your colors down!"
"I thank you, sir, perhaps after a test
I may." A British broadside brought a start
to deadly combat neither side suppressed.

1-3. Alliance vs. Atalanta and Trepassy

The sloops were lighter, faster, and with men
at sweeps, they could maneuver in a way
the brig could not. They rowed across the stern
to keep *Alliance* broadsides out of play.

A mast came crashing to the deck, and soon
the yardarm, sails and rigging came down too.
All this debris was heaved into the sea,
but still the cannon balls and grapeshot flew.

A breeze arose, and Barry turned his ship;
his guns could now resume effective fire.
Just then a grape shot struck his shoulder square
and made *Alliance* situation dire.

A sailor helped his captain go below;
a cabin had been rigged to treat those hurt.
The doctor cut the marble-sized ball out,
and though in intense pain, he was alert.

His second in command came in the room,
his ashen color showed his heightened stress.
"We've eight men dead and many wounded, shall
I strike the flag?" And although in distress

John Barry shouted "No, if this ship can't
be fought without me, carry me on deck!"
Their captain back topside inspired the crew,
their broadsides quickened, though their ship a wreck.

At three that afternoon, the British sloops
struck colors, ending Barry's painful day.
John Kessler, Barry's first mate, was dispatched
to learn who had survived the deadly fray.

He brought the *Atalanta* captain back,
and Barry met him as he came aboard.
As Captain Sampson Edwards stepped on deck,
he handed the American his sword.

When Barry handed back the sword, he said,
"You keep it, Captain, you deserve it. Please
come down with me, my cabin is below.
Now make yourself t'home – and be at ease."

Many consider John Barry to be one of the three top
American sea captains of the Revolutionary War – along
with John Paul Jones and Nelson Biddle. After the war,
Saucy Jack went on to other exploits at sea and ashore.
Despite his powerful physique, he succumbed to asthma in
1803, while the senior captain of the Navy.

2. The Battle off Flamborough Head

As John Barry brought his seamanship skills to his new country from Ireland, so too did John Paul Jones bring his skills from Scotland. In France he acquired a merchantman, ***Le Duc de Duras***, converted it to a navy ship, and renamed it ***Bonhomme Richard.*** His most notable battle was off the Yorkshire coast against the British frigate ***Serapis.***

2-1. Portrait of John Paul Jones

The Battle off Flamborough Head

John Paul, born 6 July 1747 in Arbigland, Scotland, added Jones to his surname later, and was known as Paul Jones during most of his naval career. His exploits during the Revolutionary War were many, but none so dramatic as his encounter with HMS *Serapis* in the Battle off Flamborough Head on 23 September 1779.

    *   *   *   *   *   *   *

Marooned ashore in France, mid-war, no ship
to join the fray, Paul Jones cajoled and pled
for a command. Detractors made his quest
protracted, but he always looked ahead.

When offered plodding merchantmen, he said
he wanted "no connection with a ship
that does not sail fast," he went on, "for I
intend to go in harm's way," on this trip.

At last, a French East Indian ship, *La Duc de Duras*, was available to buy.
Jones first demurred, then changed his mind and bought the ship, although it hardly pleased his eye.

Jones fitted out his ship to fight at sea,
despite the fact it lacked the speed he sought.
To honor Dr. Franklin, he renamed
his ship *Bonhomme Richard* – quite apt, he thought.

Acquiring and installing guns delayed
the preparations of the ship for sea.
His dealings with the French to get his crew
caused shipboard tensions close to mutiny.

At last, mid-August found Paul Jones at sea
commanding five ships and two privateers.
From France he headed for the Irish coast
in search of riches for his financiers.

Within a week he captured his first prize,
but also both the privateers took flight.
Then weather scattered ships of his small fleet
and fog delayed attempts to reunite.

Alliance under Captain Landais left
Jones' fleet at times to show his great disdain
for Jones – and for the fact that he had not
been named the commodore for this campaign.

Despite disloyalty and poor morale
within the other ships of his small fleet,
Jones trained the crewmen of *Bonhomme Richard,*
preparing them for the dangers they would meet.

When John Paul Jones drew plans to penetrate
the Firth of Forth and land a force ashore,
untimely shift of wind endangered ships,
frustrating his surprise attack once more.

On twenty-three September, heading north,
his fleet patrolling off the Yorkshire coast,
Jones spotted sails ahead. At once he knew:
a call for action quickly diagnosed.

A convoy from the Baltic heading south
approached Flamborough Head. In oversight
of merchantmen: one frigate and a sloop.
The hour was late, but Jones would force a fight.

The frigate was *Serapis*, fifty guns
to bear, and speed unmatched by Jones' *Richard*.
Light winds made closing slow; Jones formed his line
and flew his English colors from the yard.

As ships drew close, *Alliance* sheered away,
then *Pallas* did the same. While *Vengeance* sailed
well clear, *Richard* approached the Englishman
to port. "What ship is that?" the Captain hailed.

Jones struck the English flag and raised his own
and fired his starboard guns – a broadside round.
Serapis answered with its heavy guns.
The placid sea became a battleground.

The second salvo brought a deadly change;
a deaf'ning roar that came from decks below.
Two guns from Jones' main battery had burst,
increasing the advantage of his foe.

The dead and dying strewn around the ship,
his largest cannons silenced now for good,
Jones tried to out maneuver and confuse
the Englishman, and board him, if he could.

Serapis tried to pass ahead of Jones
and fire the broadsides Jones could not return.
But lack of wind enabled Jones to ram,
his bowsprit struck *Serapis* in the stern.

'Though battered and unable to bring guns
to bear against his foe, Jones was not through.
The English Captain called, "Has your ship struck?"
Jones' answer chilled his hurt and weary crew.

2-1. Bonhomme Richard vs. HMS Serapis

He said: "I have not yet begun to fight!"
With that he backed his topsails and pulled free;
soon both ships were again in broadside range
although *Richard* had no main battery.

Serapis lay to leeward and when wind
picked up, Jones increased speed and tried to pass ahead.
Once more, collision thwarted Jones
and turned his mizzen shrouds to tangled mass.

However, now with ship parts thus enmeshed
the ships began an eerie, deadly dance.
Richard used grappling hooks to hold them tight;
the outgunned Jones now saw he had a chance.

Serapis' guns could shoot through *Richard's* hull
but could not get to masts or guns on deck.
Richard used muskets, small guns, and grenades
to keep the English topside force in check.

The battle lasted two long hours more,
both ships awash with blood and splintered wood.
Bonhomme Richard was flooding and ablaze,
all main guns silenced long ago for good.

The piercing, choking stench of burning wood
and powder smoke stung eyes and throats alike.
As thunder of the guns made all ears ring,
Jones' crew petitioned him: "For God's sake, strike!"

Regretful of the pain and death onboard,
but John Paul Jones would never acquiesce.
When it appeared *Richard* would soon be sunk,
the main mast of *Serapis* felt the stress

of many hits and trembled with a groan,
a certain sign it could not last the night.
Serapis' captain knew his ship was lost
and tore his colors down to end the fight.

The British Captain offered Jones his sword,
but John Paul Jones would graciously decline.
He praised the Englishman for how he fought,
and then these warriors shared a glass of wine.

    * * * * * * *

The Battle off Flamborough Head was not a defining battle of the Revolutionary War. In fact, the merchant ships that *Serapis* was protecting made it safely to their destination. However, that battle provided a defining display of courage, commitment, and leadership that would echo for centuries to come among seagoing fighting men. Jones final years were spent in Paris where, in failing health, he died on July 18, 1792 at the age of 45. Buried near Paris, his remains were eventually moved to a place of honor: a sarcophagus beneath the chapel at the U. S. Naval Academy.

3. Burning of *Philadelphia*

This is the first of the remarkable exploits of Stephen Decatur documented in this book. Although still a young lieutenant when the event occurred in 1804, he gained international fame for executing one of the most daring raids in U.S. Navy history.

The Burning of *Philadelphia*

As the Quasi-War with France phased down at the opening of the 19th Century, Congress took steps to cut the Navy back to peacetime size. Numbers of ships as well as officers and enlisted men were reduced. Of the 110 lieutenants on the rolls, only 39 were retained on the active list. One of those was Lieutenant Stephen Decatur. Because of trade embargoes with England and France, the American merchants sought markets in the Mediterranean. However, the Barbary pirates from the states along the northwest coast of Africa attacked merchantmen, captured them, and took their prizes to their countries. The small American Navy could not assure safe passage for its mercantile trade; the government paid tribute to the offending countries to avoid pirating. By 1801, the bashaw of Tripoli, Yusuf Karamanli, stated that unless Washington increase the tribute paid to him, he would renounce the pact with America. Thomas Jefferson responded by sending a few more ships to the Mediterranean. The bashaw then declared war on the United States. In 1803, the Navy maintained a one-ship blockade of the Barbary port of Tripoli. The commodore of the Mediterranean squadron was Edward Preble.

* * * * * * *

October's final week brought storms with winds
that carried *Philadelphia* miles northeast
from Tripoli. But on the 31st
the ship sailed southward when the seas decreased.

Along the way, another ship was seen
ahead toward shore and heading for the bay.
But Captain William Bainbridge gave it chase;
to take a prize would make a worthwhile day.

Uncharted waters with a deep draft ship
present large risks most captains would avoid.
But Bainbridge headed shoreward in pursuit -
the first real action since he'd been deployed.

The wind did not support the speed required
to catch his prey, so to his crew's relief
the captain turned away from shore – too late.
The ship ran hard aground upon a reef.

The standard ways to lighten ship were tried
to no avail. In full view of their eyes,
the enemy saw *Philadelphia* strand.
The massive warship now became a prize.

   * * * * * * *

November 1 of 1803, a brig
named *Argus,* new, with eighteen guns, sailed in
Gibralter's port, Decatur in command;
his tour in Preble's squadron to begin.

Decatur turned command of *Argus* to
Lieutenant Isaac Hull, respected friend.
He then assumed command of *Enterprise*,
twelve guns and crew on which he could depend.

November 12th brought Preble into port
aboard his flagship, *Constitution.* He
gave orders for Decatur to meet him
in Syracuse to plan a strategy.

But twelve days hence he learned about the loss
of *Philadelphia*, changing all his plans.
His only other frigate captured, towed
to port, patched up, and in the bashaw's hands.

The scope of the disaster soon grew worse
when Preble realized they had the crew.
Three hundred hostages to sell or kill;
the bashaw had the leverage, Preble knew.

The commodore proceeded on to port
in Syracuse and met Decatur there.
A first-hand look was needed, they agreed,
before they could respond to the affair.

They put to sea and sailed in company
until approaching Tripoli midday.
The flagship stayed well out, while *Enterprise*
sailed close enough to see the entire bay.

The *Philadelphia* dwarfed the other ships;
Decatur felt a sadness at the sight.
The ship was built just blocks from where he lived;
his father its first captain – now a blight

upon the Navy, manned by enemies.
He finished observations, then returned
to make reports to Preble of the bay
defenses and the other things he learned.

Decatur volunteered to take his ship,
though small, into the harbor to attack
the captured *Philadelphia*. Preble knew
he'd likely not get ship or captain back.

Responding: "I can ill-afford to lose
another ship and crew like that," he said.
But as they started back, a sail appeared;
a four-gun ketch – the *Mastico* – ahead.

Both small and old, she looked like most the ships
along the northern coast involved in trade.
No worth as prize, but Preble and Decatur
saw it as a means to plan a raid.

The chase was short; the capture quickly made.
In Syracuse, the carpenters' report
pronounced the ship was fit. Decatur now
proposed a plan of quite a different sort.

The commodore embraced Decatur's plan
and changed the coaster to a navy ship.
Renamed *Intrepid*, it became a part
of navy history on its next trip.

    * * * * * * *

The winter seas and winds provided time
to work out all the secret plan's detail.
The risky scheme could not afford a leak;
without complete surprise, the raid would fail.

At last, on February 3rd, the sea
and wind were right to start the voyage west.
The crew of *Enterprise* had yet to learn
the plan, and what their captain would request.

Decatur outlined everything, without
ignoring things he knew would raise their fears.
Concluding, he said he would only take
with him those who were willing volunteers.

When every man and boy aboard stepped up
Decatur knew his crew had great esprit.
They walked aboard *Intrepid*, took in lines,
and unfurled sails, then headed out to sea.

    * * * * * * *

The nondescript and weatherbeaten ketch
arrived at Tripoli, late afternoon,
just thirteen days from leaving Syracuse.
Intrepid would find darkness opportune.

The topside crewmen all wore native garb;
their little ship approached the harbor guns.
But guardians of the bay would pay no heed
to ragged-looking ketch of sixty tons.

Decatur and six others walked around,
while twelve more men lay prone upon the deck.
Below were sixty armed and ready men
to anxiously await their captain's beck.

As darkness stole his view of many things,
Decatur saw the object of his quest.
Now moored in center-harbor for defense,
the *Philadelphia* towered above the rest.

Communicating now would be the job
of Salvatore Catalano, who
could speak the language of the coastal men,
and not reveal the nature of the crew.

A light breeze kept *Intrepid* on its course,
and by nine thirty, when the moon went down
they only had 200 yards to go.
They now could clearly see the lights from town.

When close abreast the massive ship, the deck
hands looking down, one ordered – Stay Away.
But Catalano said they were Maltese,
and lost an anchor in a storm that day.

He asked if he could moor along the side
just for the night; at dawn they'd go ashore
and buy new anchors. After some brief thought,
the man on deck agreed – and helped them moor.

With lines secured, the ships were pulled in close,
and when they touched, Decatur hollered, "Board!"
Decatur led his sixty well-armed men
onto the decks – no firearms – just the sword.

Surprise had been complete, the fight was fierce,
its suddenness had terrorized the crew.
Some deck hands jumped into the bay; some ran
below to hide. In minutes, it was through.

The ship belonged to the attackers, and
combustibles would start the final phase.
In gun rooms, store rooms, berth deck, cockpit, all
were quickly stocked with fuel to feed the blaze.

When all was set, Decatur gave the word
and fires were lit in all locations planned.
Then, ordering his men debark, he was
the last to leave from his attacking band.

Despite Decatur's ban on using guns,
the noise of battle in the still of night
alerted ships around – the captured ship
had been the scene of a ferocious fight.

The fire on *Philadelphia* soon was seen
by everyone awake around the bay.
Decatur knew escape required speed;
the fire had lit the harbor like mid-day.

3-2. The Burning of *Philadelphia*

Intrepid slipped the after mooring, and
the ship's boat used the forward line to tow.
They hoisted just the jib to catch the wind,
but hazards from the fire began to grow.

The holocaust consumed surrounding air
and tried to draw *Intrepid* to its side.
The oarsmen struggled till a gentle breeze
would overcome the danger to collide.

When clear of flying embers, sails unfurled,
Intrepid headed for the open sea.
The batteries ashore began to fire
a brisk barrage to thwart attempts to flee.

Intrepid's crew looked back, and saw a scene
imprinted on their minds. The orange-hued
and towering flames provided each of them
the most impressive sight they'd ever viewed.

The cannon balls came close aboard, but none
struck masts or hull. The little ship outran
the dangers; then Decatur could take stock.
Remarkably, he had not lost a man.

The voyage back to Syracuse was one
of much elation for *Intrepid*'s crew.
They'd carried out a mission without loss
that would be seen as greatest derring-do.

When Commodore Preble greeted his heroes, he threw a celebration dinner for them. He then dashed off the following letter to the Secretary of the Navy:

"Lieutenant Decatur is an officer of too much value to be neglected. The important service he has rendered in destroying an enemy's frigate of forty guns, and the gallant manner in which he performed it, in a small vessel of sixty tons and four guns, under the enemy's batteries, surrounded by their corsairs and armed boats, the crews of which stood appalled at his intrepidity and daring, would, in any navy in Europe, insure him instantaneous promotion to the rank of post captain. I wish, as a stimulus, it could be done in this instance; it would eventually be of real service to our navy. I beg earnestly to recommend him to the President that he may be rewarded according to his merit."

Stephen Decatur, twenty-five years of age, had found international fame.

4. The Attack on Tripoli

Again we find Lieutenant Stephen Decatur under the command of Edward Preble in the Mediterranean Sea, poised to make a gunboat raid on Tripoli. As in the previous poem, he faced physical combat – and succeeded.

The Attack on Tripoli

Less than six months after the burning of *Philadelphia,* August 3, 1804, Lieutenant Stephen Decatur found himself outside the harbor of Tripoli again, in charge of a small division of gunboats, in Commodore Edward Preble's Mediterranean squadron. Preble had decided to attack Tripoli despite the difficulties of attacking a well-fortified harbor, where one could not bring large ships into the fray because of water depths. His motivation was, as he put it: "to beat the Bashaw into a better humor." At this time, although neither Preble nor Decatur were aware of it, President Jefferson had already signed Decatur's new commission as captain, and it was en route to the Mediterranean.

* * * * * * *

The forces gathered outside Tripoli
included seven navy ships and eight
boats (loaned by Italy) with shallow draft.
The harbor would be hard to penetrate

with many land-based guns and tricky shoals.
The Commodore decided not to send
his squadron ships and risk a major loss.
On gunboats he decided to depend.

Group one was led by Richard Somers, while
Decatur took command to lead the other.
One boat in Somers' group was captained by
Lieutenant James Decatur, Stephen's brother.

The larger ships moved close enough to fire
at gun emplacements on the shore; meanwhile
the gunboats all advanced on ships within
the harbor, where they soon would face their trial.

4-1. Attack on Tripoli

A shift in wind took Somers out of range;
a signal error sent another back.
A third had sails shot down; it went aground.
The three boats left continued the attack.

When making their approach they fired round shot,
but once in close, each shot had musket balls
that numbered in the hundreds from each round.
Those left on deck faced boarding party brawls.

Decatur led his crew aboard a ship,
a screaming swarm with tomahawk and pike.
The pure ferocity of the attack,
the crew aboard had never seen the like.

The carnage on the deck was over soon
as many enemy jumped overboard.
Those left alive surrendered to their foe;
Decatur took his prize with bloody sword.

John Trippe attempted similar approach
but while they boarded, his boat fell away.
With just ten men he knew he had no choice;
attack or die – he led them in the fray.

Trippe and his men killed fourteen and the rest
surrendered; the Americans lost none.
Trippe split his crew to sail his captured prize
and gunboat out to sea; his work was done.

Young James Decatur made his own attack,
but his objective struck her colors fast.
But as he was to board to claim his prize,
the Turkish captain fired a single blast.

A badly wounded James fell in the bay;
his crew retrieved him, and they sailed to look
for Stephen – whom they found. His heart was racing
from the fight in which he just partook.

Enraged, Decatur sought the Turkish boat
and jumped aboard, his bloody sword in hand.
The large and swarthy captain was prepared;
a boarding pike he'd use to take his stand.

Decatur swung his sword to hit the pole,
but struck instead the metal of the pike.
His sword broke at the hilt; unarmed, he grabbed
the weapon to avoid a lethal strike.

Soon both men tumbled to the deck, engaged
in mortal combat, while the crews of each
fought furiously to save their captain's life.
One Turk found the American in reach.

He swung his scimitar, but Reuben James
absorbed the blow meant for Decatur's head.
The powerful Turk finally rolled on top
and drew a knife to strike Decatur dead.

Decatur grabbed the Turk's right wrist and held
while drawing from his pants a loaded gun.
He pressed the muzzle to the Turk's broad back
and fired. Their captain dead, the Turks were done.

Again Decatur claimed another prize,
and as the wind had shifted, a recall
was signaled by the commodore at sea.
The gunboats left the bay before nightfall.

4-2. Stephen Decatur in Combat

The victory was small, but one more step that led to forcing Tripoli to sign a treaty, ending years of naval war. Decatur now a legend in his time.

*   *   *   *   *   *   *

In the attack on Tripoli, the Americans lost no gunboats, and sustained just one fatality, James Decatur, and six wounded, including Reuben James. The bashaw of Tripoli had three gunboats sunk and three taken as prizes. They suffered 47 killed and 49 taken prisoner. The incredible courage and fighting spirit shown by Stephen Decatur and the others is difficult to match in the annals of the U.S. Navy.

5. The Birth of Old Ironsides

The first significant sea battle of the War of 1812 occurred shortly after war was declared. Captain Isaac Hull commanded *Constitution* in the encounter with the British frigate *Guerriere*. The events of the battle led to *Constitution* earning the nickname Old Ironsides.

5-1. Portrait of Isaac Hull

The Birth of Old Ironsides

In July of 1812, a month after the United States had declared war on the British Empire, Captain Isaac Hull took command of USS *Constitution*, a ship he had served in earlier in his career. Having taken on stores in Annapolis, the ship cleared the Virginia Capes and headed north to join a squadron headed by Commodore John Rodgers. Meanwhile, the British in Halifax, upon learning of the war declaration, deployed its own squadron of four warships, commanded by Captain Philip Broke, to find and attack Rodgers. HMS *Guerriere,* commanded by Captain James Richard Dacres, joined the British squadron en route.

* * * * * * *

Inbound toward New York Hull sighted sails
of five ships to the east and heading west.
His ship becalmed, night falling fast, he raised
light signals, an identifying test.

Receiving no reply he made no move
to close, but maintained caution through the night.
When day broke he could see five British ships
approaching with intent to force a fight.

Soon all ships had no wind to fill their sails;
the range was still too great to use their guns.
Hull used his boats to tow his ship away,
and pumped fresh water out – about ten tons.

The British tried to use their boats the same,
but *Constitution* kept just out of range.
With shallow water, Hull began to kedge,
and soon the tactic caused his lead to change.

The slow-paced chase, where oars replaced the sails
continued for three long and tedious days.
A gentle breeze reached *Constitution* first,
and now the chase began a second phase.

As Hull watched anxiously, his sails began
to fill, and *Constitution* came alive.
Its greater speed left all five British ships
behind; the U.S. ship would now survive.

When out of sight, Hull changed his course and made
for Boston harbor's safety and supplies.
His stay there short, he headed up the coast
off Newfoundland to seek a British prize.

Hull sank two British merchantmen, and then
turned south. He ran across a privateer
that passed the news that they had just outrun
a British frigate operating near.

This was the information Hull had sought,
and so, at his best speed, the search began.
On August nineteenth, two o'clock, "Sail ho!"
aroused the pulse of every fighting man.

While *Constitution* had the wind, Hull closed,
until within three miles where he could see
his contact was the frigate *Guerriere*.
The battle Hull had wished for now would be.

As Hull reduced the range, the British ship
launched several broadsides; Hull held fire instead.
A British cannon ball bounced off the ship.
"The sides are made of iron," one man said.

5-2. USS Constitution vs. HMS Guerriere

That statement made in heated battle led
to legend that survived to present day.
But Captain Isaac Hull would make his fame
by leaving enemies in disarray.

Lieutenant Morris, second in command,
three times requested Hull to loose his guns.
Each time Hull held him back until they reached
that close-in killing range where no one runs.

Abreast at twenty-five yards, Hull let go
with cannon ball and grape shot, three quick rounds.
He crossed ahead and freed the other side;
the air was filled with awesome battle sounds.

The gunsmoke made it difficult to breathe,
and hard to even see the enemy.
An elevated broadside shredded sails
and tossed the mizzen mast into the sea.

Hull tried to cross the bow again, but was
too close to *Guerriere*. Her bowsprit caught
in *Constitution*'s rigging, which could lead
to boarding party battles to be fought.

While musket fire kept boarders laying low,
both ships still fired their cannons as they could.
A shot took down the British foremast, and
it dragged the mainmast, splintering the wood.

Both ships were shaken, causing them to part.
As *Constitution* moved away to rake
the British ship once more, the *Guerriere*
fired once – away – she'd had all she could take.

The signal of surrender was made thus,
because the ship no longer had a mast.
From when Hull ordered broadsides to begin
until the end, just one half hour had passed.

Lieutenant George Read was dispatched by Hull
to board his foe and see what he could learn.
Read stepped across the deck made slick by blood,
requesting Captain Dacres to return

with him by boat to meet with Captain Hull.
When Captain Dacres offered Hull his sword,
Hull graciously declined. To keep his prize
afloat, he sent a crew to go aboard.

Next afternoon, they realized the ship
could not be saved; the prize crew was returned.
The captured sailors transferred by long boat
to *Constitution,* where some facts were learned.

Ten sailors found in *Guerriere* had been
impressed from a U. S. ship while ashore.
Ironically, this was a major cause
for the United States to declare war.

Once everyone was clear of *Guerriere,*
Hull ordered it blown up – destroyed at sea.
One battle – one ship sunk – to celebrate
as Isaac Hull could savor victory.

One British frigate lost could hardly be
a devastating loss to such a fleet.
But still, morale throughout the country soared;
the taste of victory indeed was sweet.

      *   *   *   *   *   *   *

The victory of *Constitution* over *Guerriere* made Isaac Hull a national hero, and began a rebuilding of national confidence in the American Navy. Subsequent successes would support this confidence. "Old Ironsides" would be pressed into important service very soon after this battle, but under a new captain: William Bainbridge.

6. Macedonian Meets United States

This is the most significant one-on-one battle fought by Commodore Stephen Decatur during the War of 1812. As commanding officer of *United States* he engaged the British frigate *Macedonian* near Cape Verde Isles.

6-1. Portrait of Stephen Decatur

Macedonian Meets United States

In June of 1812, the British Navy consisted of over 600 ships, including 124 ships of the line (with over 60 guns each) and 116 frigates (with 28 to 50 guns). The United States Navy had three large frigates (44 guns) and three standard frigates (38 guns). The British mounted over 20,000 guns; the Americans had fewer than 450. Despite this clear disparity, with the political situation badly deteriorated, the American Congress declared war on Great Britain that month.

* * * * * * *

The day was clear; the breeze blew from southeast.
United States patrolled alone to hunt
for British ships to fight or else, perhaps,
a richly laden merchant to confront.

October 25 of 1812,
the ship cruised near Cape Verde Isles. The crew
had Commodore Decatur in command;
his battle reputation they all knew.

Just past sunrise, the crow's nest came alive –
"Sail ho!" resounded from above; replied
the officer on deck: "and where away?"
"Hull down, broad off the larboard side."

Decatur changed his course to south-southwest;
his sailing master raised more sail to speed
the intercept. Identifying what
the ship was would define how to proceed.

Though battle stations need not be manned yet,
the crew began collecting on the deck.
Prepared and trained for action as they were,
they gave their guns just one more final check.

When range was under seven miles, they saw
the ship had three masts; now they must assume
a British warship – battle stations now.
A drummer's cadence sounded: boom – boom – boom.

The well-drilled crew went through familiar steps:
They opened ports; cast loose the guns; and ran
them out. They brought supplies from magazines
supporting gunfire once the fight began.

All guns were loaded, double shots, prepared
to fire. While pistol, cutlass, boarding pikes
were stashed topside, marines climbed masts to add
their musket fire, when close enough to strike.

When guns were seen, Decatur turned his ship
to gain the weather gauge. The stranger turned
to thwart the move, but showed its single deck:
a frigate; whose? Decatur quickly learned.

The frigate raised the Union Jack. A cheer
went up; Decatur hoisted Stars and Stripes.
By now the ships were side by side, about
a mile apart, and similar in types.

United States' first broadside round fell short,
but being double shot, Decatur gauged
with single shot he was in range. He called
the order: "Fire at will!" The battle raged.

Decatur and his first lieutenant had
discussed their strategy, and both agreed:
attack the topside – sails and rigging first.
A ship that can't maneuver can't succeed.

The pace of gunfire raised an acrid cloud
that hid the ships at times and choked the crew.
Each broadside made the ship recoil and sway;
his gun crews would prevail, Decatur knew.

The concentration on the topside masts
began to tell – the mizzen first to go.
One gunner called: "We've made a brig of her!"
Decatur, looking for a lethal blow,

called back: "Aim at the mainmast, and she'll be
a sloop." Just minutes later, gunners scored
a hit that brought the mainmast crashing down
into the fore topmast. Now all onboard

the British frigate knew their damage was
extensive but they still fought on. Now near
enough to bring the carronades to bear,
the British braced for onslaught more severe.

Then unexpectedly, the shelling stopped;
United States pulled off its crippled foe.
The British failed to understand the move,
but used the time to get those hurt below.

Decatur hove to when two miles away,
and then explained his actions to his men.
"They're beaten, but don't recognize it yet.
Let's give them time; we'll go back in and then,

if they reject surrender, we'll resume.
Remember, without sails they cannot run."
Upon returning to close range, they viewed
the Union Jack come down – the battle won.

6-2. USS United States vs. HMS Macedonian

"What ship is this?" Decatur shouted out.
The answer brought fulfillment quite unplanned.
"His Majesty's ship, Macedonian"
and "Captain John S. Carden in command."

A few long months ago, before the war,
John Carden visited United States.
Decatur hosted him, and they discussed
the strange things war could bring, and if the fates

placed them in combat, ship-on-ship, who would
emerge with victory. They disagreed
with friendly banter, but they never thought
the question would be answered with such speed.

Decatur sent his prize crew to effect
repairs so he could justly claim his prize.
It took five days to plug the holes and raise
a mizzen mast. Unpleasant to the eyes,

but it could sail. The journey they endured:
in excess of two thousand miles. More than
a month it took to reach New London's base.
Again Decatur was the hero-man.

* * * * * * *

This victory, coupled with Isaac Hull's defeat of *Guerriere,* raised the country's morale and gained a measure of acceptance of "Mr. Madison's War."

7. Constitution Versus Java

Nine years after William Bainbridge ran *Philadelphia* aground off the coast of Tripoli and languished as a prisoner of the bashaw of Tripoli, he found himself in command of Old Ironsides. He had been reinstated as a captain, and sought to erase the blemish on his record by heroic actions in combat. His encounter with the British frigate *Java* provided that opportunity.

7-1. Portrait of William Bainbridge

Constitution Versus Java

Shortly after *Constitution* returned to Boston after Isaac Hull's victory over *Guerriere*, a change of command placed William Bainbridge in command of Old Ironsides. Bainbridge had been in command of *Philadelphia* when it ran aground and was captured by Tripoli. He was anxious to get to sea and find action that would erase the blemish on his record from years before. *Constitution* embarked from Boston on October 26, 1812 with *Hornet* (James Lawrence in command) in company.

* * * * * * *

The voyage to the South Atlantic went
without event; the search for British ships
began. What Bainbridge sought was victory
that other captains' glory would eclipse.

When off Bahia, a Brazilian port,
they found *Bonne Citoyenne* moored overnight.
A sloop, it was a match for *Hornet*'s size,
so Lawrence sent a challenge for a fight.

Bonne Citoyenne refused to take the dare,
so Bainbridge ordered *Hornet* to remain
and block the port, preventing an escape.
Then Bainbridge left to start his hunt again.

December 29, two ships were seen
approaching *Constitution* from the east.
They had the wind with them, so Bainbridge slowed,
prepared for battle as the range decreased.

The British frigate *Java* was the type
of foe that Bainbridge hoped that he would meet.
But *Java*'s captain, Henry Lambert, planned
avenging *Guerriere*'s erstwhile defeat.

The second ship, a captured merchantman,
would play no role in battle soon to start.
As *Java* closed the range, both ships reduced
their sails – now just three hundred yards apart.

As *Constitution* opened broadside fire
and *Java* answered with effective blasts.
The faster *Java* tried to edge ahead,
but Bainbridge increased sails upon his masts.

Now at close range and matching speeds, both ships
exchanged broadsides with damaging effect.
One British cannonball blew off the wheel
and ended steering by the helm direct.

The *Constitution* crew worked under fire
to rig lines from the rudder to regain
control. Now Lambert turned his ship to close
with the intent to board and thus attain

advantage with his many troops. The use
of grapeshot made the *Java* deck a place
where many died, some masts were splintered, and
the sails began to look like wind-blown lace.

The *Java* bowsprit caught the rigging aft
and soon broke off, the jib boom also fell.
Then a marine, with a clear musket shot,
dropped Captain Lambert with one well-aimed shell.

The furious battle now was near its end
as *Java*'s fore and mizzen masts were lost.
The wounded Bainbridge pulled his frigate clear
to make repairs and to assess the cost

7-2. USS *Constitution* vs. HMS *Java*

in lives the battle caused. There was no doubt
that *Java* could not run – and while apart
the damaged mainmast tumbled to the sea.
A British sailor showed his fighting heart

by hoisting Union Jack on one mast stub.
When *Constitution* moved in to resume
the battle, *Java* struck her colors. Joy
broke out on one ship, on the other – gloom.

The prize crew boarding *Java* were appalled
by all the damage and the carnage there.
Lieutenant General Thomas Hislop was
a passenger caught in a sudden snare.

He was en route to India to assume
the role of governor – but not for now.
A prisoner, he knew his future must
depend on what his captors would allow.

Since *Constitution* was so far from home,
and Bainbridge wanted *Java* as his prize,
repairs were made, but little could be done.
The first rough seas and *Java* would capsize.

On New Year's Eve of 1812, the crew
of *Java* and the prize crew were returned.
The British derelict was set ablaze;
the *Java* crew looked on as their ship burned.

In three days Captain Lambert died of wounds,
and Bainbridge sailed his ship to U. S. shore.
He, too, now had a famous wartime win;
"Old Ironsides" victorious once more.

8. "Don't Give Up the Ship..."

Having completed a successful cruise commanding *Hornet*, Lieutenant James Lawrence was promoted and assigned to command *Chesapeake*, then fitting out in Boston. When the ship was ready for sea, Lawrence hastily took on stores and ammunition and put to sea to engage *Shannon* in an early tragedy of the war.

8-1. Portrait of James Lawrence

"Don't Give Up The Ship..."

In the first few months of the War of 1812, that began in June of that year, naval strategies were formed through necessity. The United States Navy consisted of very few ships; the British Navy was a world-wide power. If the British saw the U.S. as a serious at-sea threat, they could have crushed the threat with overwhelming force; they didn't. The early successes of Hull and Decatur demonstrated that evenly matched, one-on-one engagements could lead to stunning outcomes that raised the country's morale and made national heroes of the captains. The strategy included avoiding hazarding one's ship in encounters with more than one enemy ship, but seeking engagements with equals. Contemporaries of Hull and Decatur sought to match their success. Some who tried did not succeed, but still became lasting parts of history

* * * * * * *

On 26 October, 1812,
the frigate *Constitution* sailed away
from Boston heading for the trade routes south,
with *Hornet* leaving Boston the same day.

With Captain William Bainbridge in command,
the frigate and the sloop joined up at sea.
James Lawrence, in command of *Hornet*, had
his orders: follow Bainbridge's lead and be

an escort as they sailed to rendezvous
with *Essex* somewhere near Cape Verde Isles.
When *Essex* failed to show, they went on south
in search of prey, they'd travel many miles.

Lieutenant Lawrence drilled his *Hornet*'s crew
while transiting the South Atlantic sea.
When off Bahia, Captain Bainbridge saw
a British sloop, *Bonne Citoyenne*, and he

was certain that the sloop would never leave
with *Constitution* waiting to attack.
He left the sloop for *Hornet* to await,
departing to resume his southern track.

With *Constitution* gone, James Lawrence sent
a written challenge to the ship in port
to put to sea and battle one-on-one.
The captain of the sloop would not abort

his mission loading quantities of coins.
To thwart the sloop's escape, James Lawrence set
a one-ship blockade of Bahia's port.
He'd wait to trap the prize within his net.

However, when a British man-of-war
was spotted heading in, the blockade broke.
The *Hornet* captain knew he was out-gunned;
he searched for even battles to provoke.

In time he found *Peacock*, a British sloop;
he made a fast approach with guns all clear.
The battle was one-sided; *Hornet*'s guns
struck *Peacock*'s hull with damage so severe

it sank just fifteen minutes from the start.
Survivors were collected and embarked
in *Hornet*. Lawrence headed for New York,
where his success in battle quickly sparked

a hero's welcome and promotion too.
Now Captain Lawrence had a new command.
He went to Boston to join *Chesapeake*,
completing overhaul and being manned.

* * * * * * *

Late May, 1813

Just outside Boston lurked two men-of-war,
intending to prevent ships leaving port.
HMS *Shannon* under Philip Broke
had *Tenedos* to serve as an escort.

Broke was well-known for skill in gunnery;
his ship a match in guns with *Chesapeake*.
He knew that ship would soon prepare to sail;
this was a battle he would surely seek.

It was just two weeks earlier that fog
engulfed the coast; low visibility
helped *President* and *Congress* to avoid
the blockade and sail safely out to sea.

Detaching *Tenedos*, Broke sent a note
inviting *Chesapeake* to come ahead
and meet with *Shannon* – battle one-on-one:
a challenge Captain Lawrence never read.

* * * * * * *

James Lawrence had an urge to follow up
his *Peacock* victory with more success.
He knew command of *Chesapeake* would give
him opportunities he could finesse.

When he learned *Shannon* was outside the port,
alone and standing ready to engage
departing ships, he felt this was his chance;
this was a battle he would have to wage.

Expecting that support for *Shannon* might
arrive, his preparation time was short.
Supplies and crew were hastily acquired;
at noon, the first of June, he sailed from port.

The British ship stood out to sea to wait
for *Chesapeake*'s engagement to begin.
Broke said: "Fire into quarters ... Kill the men ...
the ship is yours..." He taught them how to win.

At nearly six o'clock, as *Chesapeake*
caught up, the chance to turn and rake was passed;
instead she drew up on the starboard side
of *Shannon*. Broadside time had come at last.

The ships in parallel at pistol range
began the fight with devastating fire.
Grenades and muskets with the cannon rounds
created on-deck situation dire.

Two-thirds of *Chesapeake*'s crew out on deck
were felled, including Captain Lawrence, who
sustained a painful leg wound early on.
Both hulls were holed with rigging damage too.

The British gunners had done better work
but neither ship could keep a steady course.
They came together accidentally,
and each ships called away its boarding force.

James Lawrence, in full uniform, was shot,
by musket fire by a marine. When he
was being carried down below, he stopped
and uttered words that would make history.

This captain, who believed in openness,
and letting crewmen know just what he thinks,
called: "Tell the men ... fire faster. Don't give up
the ship! (and added) Fight her till she sinks."

8-2. USS *Chesapeake* vs. HMS *Shannon*

Inspired, his crew fought on but hopelessly.
The crew below decks tried to join the fray,
but musket fire down hatches ended that.
The battle ended; *Shannon* won the day.

This battle lasted just a quarter hour.
The British boarding party had been led
by *Shannon* captain Philip Broke, himself,
who suffered from a badly wounded head.

The British victor, with its prize, made way
for Halifax, with Lawrence failing fast.
He died at sea, but not his memory;
this sailor was courageous to the last.

   *   *   *   *   *   *   *

Captain Broke recovered from his wounds, was knighted, and promoted to Rear Admiral. However, he never went to sea again. James Lawrence's body was returned to the United States, and is buried in the yard at Trinity Church in New York. Lawrence's dynamic words were heeded. It was not until the surviving members of *Chesapeake*'s crew were captured that a British captor lowered the ship's colors; James Lawrence's crew did not "give up the ship."

9. The Battle of Lake Erie

General William Henry Harrison found that his efforts to prosecute the war in the northwest was hampered by the British controlling Lake Erie. In 1813, Oliver Hazard Perry was assigned to build and command a fleet on the lake, and gain control of Lake Erie.

9-1. Portrait of Oliver Hazard Perry

The Battle of Lake Erie

In early 1813, Oliver Hazard Perry sought a more active role in the war and was reassigned from command of a gunboat flotilla in Newport to direct the American naval effort on Lake Erie. At the time, there were no naval forces on Lake Erie; the British controlled the lake. The American land forces could not succeed in the west while the British controlled Lake Erie.

* * * * * * *

An unencumbered line where sea met sky,
the lookout scanned about with watchful eye.
September morning's beauty went unseen,
for Captain Perry knew the day would bring
both challenges and pain of battle's sting;
his course was clear – let nothing intervene.

On deck he mused, *How would they meet the test?*
The times for building, training were compressed.
Just eight short months since Presque Isle first he saw,
no ships, no crew, a massive task at hand:
Secure Lake Erie; make it your command,
defeat the British; force them to withdraw.

* * * * * * *

A shipwright, Noah Brown, began to build
the ships with many workers barely skilled.
As wintry blasts slowed building more than planned,
throughout the backwoods camps the Captain went
recruiting volunteers to complement
the corps of crew assigned to his command.

Captain Perry named his flagship for
James Lawrence, killed just three short months before.
A sky-blue battle banner raised with pride,
emblazoned with the hero's final phrase,
those words that made the fighting spirit blaze:
Don't give up the ship, he'd said – and died.

Mid-summer came, construction was complete;
the untrained crews were drilled in August heat.
Two brigs with twenty guns, and smaller craft
comprised the fleet; with **Lawrence** in the lead,
Niagara close behind with matching speed;
remaining smaller ships fell in abaft.

Among the crew was Perry's brother James,
a midshipman who shared his lofty aims.
Though pleased to have the youth beside him now,
the captain feared in battles to arise,
he might be forced to witness James' demise,
but midshipmen must pass this test somehow.

* * * * * * *

The British squadron on Lake Erie bore
its long-range guns aboard six men-of-war.
One-armed Robert Barclay was in charge,
(he'd been among Lord Nelson's retinue)
Detroit his flagship, battle-tested crew.
Captain Perry's task was looming large.

* * * * * * *

The battle group sailed west, the hunt began;
for days the lack of wind delayed their plan.
Despite increasing sail, the pace was slow.
Though boredom seized the crew, this soon would change
whenever British ships would come in range.
The early morning silence broke, *Sail Ho!*

The flagship *Lawrence*, leading, turned to close
and sorted through the foe to juxtapose.
Above the midday breeze, a fateful sound
when Rule Britannia drifted from *Detroit*.
This motivated Perry to exploit
his battle skills, his rival to confound.

As Perry moved his ship through heavy fire
while standing tall, his forces to inspire,
maneuvering to bring *Detroit* abeam.
With gun-for-gun and man-for-man they fought,
with brave men dying under the onslaught.
Their boldness, strength, and courage were the theme.

The boom – boom – boom of cannon numbed the ear,
while acrid smell of smoke made nostrils sear;
hot powder's stinging lashes singed the face.
The sight of fallen comrades on the deck,
with gaping wounds to body, head, and neck
made hardened warriors cringe without disgrace.

The smoke of battle crept across the lake
at gunwale level, putrid and opaque;
each breath brought bitter pungent tang to taste.
But battle on they did as best they could,
their numbers dwindled, but they understood
no greater test had any crewman faced.

Within two hours, only twenty stood,
while eighty-three stout hearts were stopped for good.
When *Lawrence* had its final gun destroyed,
the Captain, brother James, plus four men more
rowed on to board *Niagara* to restore
their leader to a ship to be deployed.

9-2. The Battle of Lake Erie

Niagara sailed into the fray with verve,
its cheering crew held nothing in reserve.
Their weary foe now short of man and gun;
with Perry's hard-fought vict'ry all but sealed,
the badly wounded Barclay forced to yield,
the battle ended; Perry's mission done.

When all the captured ships had been secured,
and his small fleet still floating, safely moored,
the Captain penned his terse report that said:
We have met the enemy; he wrote
and they are ours. Two ships, two brigs, (his note
went on) *one schooner, and one sloop* (it read).

As Captain Perry praised his gallant men,
he comforted the wounded once again.
Though death had taken many of his crew,
he thanked the Lord his brother was alive.
The boy, but twelve, was lucky to survive.
He smiled at James and said, *We've much to do!*

   * * * * * * *

Oliver Hazard Perry's victory enabled the American military to regain control of the northwest. His brief message to General William Henry Harrison became as famous in navy annals as his battle flag. The battle was the only instance in British naval history where an entire squadron was surrendered. After the war, in 1819, while on a diplomatic mission in South America for President Monroe, Oliver Hazard Perry contracted yellow fever and died at age 34.

10. The Final Cruise of *Essex*

The 13-year old *Essex* began its final voyage in late 1812, under the command of David Porter. A plan to rendezvous with **Constitution** in the South Atlantic was aborted and Porter took his ship to the Pacific to raid British merchantmen. He yearned for a one-on-one battle with a British frigate, but was forced into a one-on-two encounter at the Battle of Valparaiso.

The Final Cruise of USS *Essex*

USS *Essex* was built in Salem, Massachusetts (Essex County) for $74,000, money pledged to the government by the people of Salem. It was launched on 30 September 1799 as a 32-gun frigate. Through its life as a U.S. Navy ship, it had many interesting, though not spectacular cruises, but featured commanding officers of significant repute: Edward Preble, William Bainbridge, James Barron, and David Porter. Its final voyage as a Navy ship, under the command of David Porter, ended at the historic battle at Valparaiso, Chile on March 28, 1814.

* * * * * * *

The second cruise of David Porter's tour
commanding *Essex* started in the fall
of 1812, October 29.
Despite his strong objections, long guns, all

but six, replaced by short-range carronades.
Though powerful at close-in range, he would
be disadvantaged, for a British ship
would stay at long range, if indeed it could.

His orders were to voyage to the South
Atlantic and to make a rendezvous
with *Constitution* there, then hunt and fight
all British men-of-war they could pursue.

When Porter searched the sea lanes of the South
Atlantic, he found neither enemy
nor friendly ships around. He then moved on
to find another meeting place at sea.

Again without success, he took his ship
five hundred miles due south of Rio, where
the final meeting place had been defined.
A Portuguese ship was encountered there.

Its crew related how a U.S. ship
had fought and sunk a British man-of-war.
(The *Constitution-Java* battle was
the incident that happened weeks before.)

This welcome news led Porter to surmise
that *Constitution* was the U.S. ship.
He knew the British fleet would scour the sea
and he would need to find a way to slip

away from them; his orders now were moot.
He reasoned that if he could round the Horn,
his ship could capture British merchantmen,
collecting cargoes that were ocean borne.

In January 1813, when
the roiling killer seas and vicious gales
had terrorized the *Essex* crew, they learned
the Cape Horn legends weren't just sailors' tales.

However, once the passage was complete,
the ship began its grand Pacific cruise.
For twelve long months it raided British ships;
the whaling industry had much to lose.

Eleven ships in all were *Essex* prey,
but Porter sought a battle one-on-one
against a British frigate near his size:
a ship that he could equal, gun for gun.

In February 1814, he
took *Essex* into Valparaiso Bay.
A British frigate and a sloop-of-war
sailed in the harbor on another day.

Although a neutral harbor, tensions rose
as enemies at war came face-to-face.
Both sides prepared for battle, but none came;
the captains honored Chile's neutral space.

HMS *Phoebe* was the larger ship,
and *Cherub* was the sloop in company.
Commanding *Phoebe*, Captain Hillyar had
his orders not to let the *Essex* flee.

Both captains were experienced and knew
each other from the pre-war days long gone.
They dined and socialized as if close friends,
but both were sure they soon would meet head-on.

The Porter plan was goad his former friend
into a *Phoebe-Essex* one-on-one.
But Hillyar would not jeopardize his goal:
ensure that *Essex* raiding days were done.

The bantering between the foes kept on
with Porter voicing challenges anew.
When asked what he would do with captured ships,
he threatened to destroy a prize or two.

Hillyar replied, "Not while I am in sight."
A few days later, Porter followed through.
He towed two captured British ships to sea
and set them both ablaze in Hillyar's view.

Despite this provocation, Hillyar still
refused to send the sloop away and fight
the type of battle Porter sought. He kept
his ships on station, blocking *Essex* flight.

For seven weeks the stand-off had gone on,
when weather proved to be the stalemate's flaw.
A sudden wind struck *Essex* with the strength
to part an anchor cable. Porter saw

his ship was being pushed toward open sea;
the other anchor could not overcome
the force that seemed intent on leaving him
exposed to British guns he'd hidden from.

Decision time was on him, Porter knew,
and now the opportunity to flee
was his best course; he rigged his sails for speed.
His ship was faster than his enemy.

Just as he rounded Angel's Point, the ship
was greeted by a sudden, raging squall.
He could not furl his sails in time to save
the main topmast, its halyards, sails and all.

The loss of sail meant he could not outrun
the British ships, nor could he make it back
to Valparaiso. Porter sought a bay
where he would be immune from an attack.

He found Viña del Mar and anchored there,
protected by neutrality, he thought.
However, *Phoebe* and the sloop bore down;
he cleared the decks; a battle would be fought.

10-1. USS *Essex* Facing HMS *Phoebe* and HMS *Cherub*

As *Cherub* closed on *Essex* first, she fired
a broadside, then took station off the bow.
Arriving shortly after, *Phoebe* took her place
astern, at distance long guns would allow.

With just his few 12-pounders that would reach
the British, Porter's gunners showed their skill.
In half an hour, both the British ships
pulled back to make repairs. All guns were still

while damage was assessed. The mainsail, jib,
and mainstay, all of *Phoebe,* had been hit.
In *Cherub*, Captain Tucker had sustained
severe wounds, but fought on in spite of it.

The British moved in for the kill, but stayed
well clear of carronade range once again.
The many British guns filled *Essex* hull
with holes; its decks were slick with bloody stain.

The pounding cannon balls crunched wooden decks
and leashed the deadly four-foot splinter spears.
As gun crews died on deck they were replaced
by gallant men who fought despite their fears.

Although the damage to his ship extreme,
the captain got the *Essex* under way
and moved against the British to attack.
Just one broadside, and *Cherub* backed away.

With *Phoebe* wisely keeping distance that
its long guns could continue their attack,
while *Essex* could not close enough to board,
and short-range carronades could not fire back.

With his attack plan thwarted, he turned 'round
and headed *Essex* straight for Chilean shore.
He hoped to scuttle ship and thus avoid
surrendering his ship in time of war.

However, once again the weather played
a role defeating Porter's final try.
An offshore wind moved *Essex* back to face
a raking fire – and he could not reply.

With death and pain around him, Porter knew
his ship would soon be sunk with all aboard.
Reluctantly, he hauled his colors down,
a battle-ending action he abhorred.

For two and one half hours the battle raged
with *Essex* being pounded by long guns.
Its death toll would exceed one hundred souls,
and many scarred for life: the wounded ones.

This ended *Essex* fifteen year career:
the U.S. Navy ship with honored past.
It had survived exciting times at sea,
but none so devastating as its last.

    * * * * * * *

Essex was patched up, having absorbed 50 broadsides, and taken to England. David Porter and his surviving crew (including his foster son, Midshipman David Glasgow Farragut) were paroled and made their way back to United States. Eventually, Porter returned home after being away for a year and a half. There he met his son, David Dixon Porter, for the first time. Later, David Porter served on the first Board of Navy Commissioners, along with John Rodgers and Isaac Hull. In his final federal service, David Porter was appointed chargé d'affaires at Constantinople by President Jackson, where he served from 1831 until his death of heart failure in 1843.

11. The Battle of Lake Champlain

In 1814, while the war with England was not going well, the new government realized it was vulnerable to attack from the north. Thomas Macdonough was given the assignment to build a force on Lake Champlain that would thwart an attack from Canada. The outcome was one of the most significant battles of the War of 1812.

11-1. Portrait of Thomas Macdonough

The Battle of Lake Champlain

By 1814, the War of 1812 was not going well, and the future of the young country was in question. In August, British troops had marched on Washington, sending the government into hiding and burning the Capitol and the White House. However, in September, a battle took place in Lake Champlain, just off Plattsburgh, New York, that changed the complexion of the war. More than 100 years later, Winston Churchill would refer to it as "the most decisive engagement of the war."

*   *   *   *   *   *   *

"Command of what? A fleet that isn't there,"
exclaimed Macdonough from his gunboat's deck.
The messenger replied, "I'm sorry, sir."
"It's not your fault, but I shall have to check."

Lieutenant Tom Macdonough took command
of Portland's gunboats just four weeks before.
This shift in orders caught him by surprise,
but he knew how plans change when you're at war.

He sensed a major task would lie ahead;
the fleet at Lake Champlain did not exist.
A battle-tested veteran that he was –
his gunboat building time had not been missed.

In Autumn 1812, Macdonough left
the rocky shores of Maine for Lake Champlain.
Strategic value of the lake was clear;
a firm control of it he must maintain.

Vergennes, Vermont was chosen as the spot
to set about the building of his fleet.
With Noah Brown, the shipwright from New York,
Macdonough set a schedule he must meet.

Recruiting men, then training them to fight,
became the major work for months on end.
He learned a British frigate being built
would compromise his efforts to defend.

Macdonough made appeals for funds to build
a larger ship; at last his needs were met.
Authority to build a sloop of war
enabled him to face the British threat.

   * * * * * * *

In Spring of 1814, large-scale change,
with war in France no longer a concern,
Napoleon was off to Elba Isle,
and many British soldiers could return.

Instead, the British government would hatch
a secret scheme supporting long-range plans.
The British troops in France, now not engaged,
would be dispatched to fight Americans.

Ten thousand battle-tested soldiers left
from France to join the forces in Quebec.
Invasion by the Hudson and Lake George
required that Lake Champlain not bottleneck.

Combined assault by land and lake was planned,
the troops would march to Plattsburg with great haste.
The Royal Navy ships would meet them there,
destroying any war ships that they faced.

The War Department sent the Army west
despite the danger lurking to the north.
Now Plattsburgh's fort could not resist attack;
invasion then commenced September 4th.

September 7th, 1814 marked
the day the British captured Plattsburgh's fort.
Macdonough knew that soon George Downie's fleet
would make the rendezvous he was to thwart.

   * * * * * * *

As Thomas Macdonough recognized that his confrontation with the British was just days away, he was able to bring fourteen ships to bear: *Saratoga*, his flagship, a sloop of war; *Eagle*, a brig; *Ticonderoga*, a schooner; *Preble*, a converted merchantman; 5 galleys; and 5 gunboats. His adversary, Captain George Downie, commanded fifteen ships: *Confiance*, his flagship, a frigate (the largest and most heavily armed ship on the lake); *Linnet*, a brig; *Chub*, a converted merchantman; *Finch*, a converted merchantman; and 11 gunboats.

   * * * * * * *

Macdonough used his knowledge of the lake
and understanding of the British plan
to pick the point where battle would be waged;
he'd be in place before the fight began.

He brought his fleet inside the harbor mouth
at Plattsburgh, in the lee of Cumberland Head.
With all sails furled they formed a north-south line
and anchored with the major ships ahead.

When situated where he wished to be,
Macdonough dropped his anchors fore and aft.
He had kedge anchors towed away and dropped;
his ship was now a stable fighting craft.

His seamanship had one more benefit;
if needed he could move his ship around.
With sails furled he could still rotate his ship,
and thus his adversaries to confound.

The gunboats and the galleys were behind
and at line ends so British ships could not
avoid Macdonough's battle line now formed.
They prayed that they could foil the British plot.

Eleventh of September, early morn
brought Downie's fleet within Macdonough's view.
A shifting wind decreased the fleet's advance,
requiring patience from the nervous crew.

George Downie planned to sail his frigate through
the line between the *Saratoga*'s bow
and *Eagle*'s stern and anchor there to rake
both ships with fire; escape he'd not allow.

Some early shots by *Eagle* and *Linnet*
fell short, but as the *Confiance* drew near,
Macdonough fired his favorite gun, and struck
the frigate's bow and swept its gun deck clear.

Macdonough's ships then opened heavy fire
with Downie's flagship taking many hits.
The first barrage sliced topside rigging up
and blew the larboard anchors into bits.

The damage ended Downie's plan to break
Macdonough's line. He anchored, furled his sails,
and opened fire. Some thirty cannon balls
slammed *Saratoga*'s hull beneath the rails.

The flagship shuddered; many sailors died.
Though blood and splintered wood lay all about,
the fight went on. One ball took out a boom
and snapped the spar that knocked their captain out.

11-2. Victory at Lake Champlain

In seconds he awoke, then rallied troops
and manned his gun. A *Saratoga* shot
dislodged a midships gun in *Confiance*.
The three-ton, cast iron cannon left its spot

and landed on the British commodore.
The battle was just fifteen minutes old
when Captain Downie lost his life on deck.
James Robertson took charge when he was told.

Meanwhile, *Linnet* and *Chubb* sailed toward the line;
attack the northern flank was their intent.
But Robert Henley's *Eagle* was prepared
to vanquish any ships the British sent.

Linnet and *Eagle* traded shots while *Chubb*
positioned ship to fire on *Eagle*'s bow.
Then *Eagle* concentrated heavy guns
on *Chubb*, its planned assault to disallow.

Chubb drifted like a derelict amid
the ships wherein the heated battle raged.
Eventually, the injured captain struck;
now from the battle, *Chubb* was disengaged.

The action at the southern end became
intense when *Finch* and British gunboats made
attacks on *Preble* and *Ticonderoga*.
But, *Preble* buckled in the fusillade.

She slipped her anchor and retired toward shore,
her colors struck. Now *Finch* turned its attack
upon *Ticonderoga,* which had been
engaging British gunboats without slack.

Ticonderoga focused fire on *Finch*,
and put five holes below its waterline.
Finch drifted toward Crab Island, went aground,
and helpless now, struck colors to resign.

Linnet and *Confiance* were still engaged
with *Eagle* and Macdonough's flagship, and
each ship sustaining many hits, the dead
and injured mounted, testing each command.

A shot from *Linnet* tore an anchor spring
line, forcing *Eagle*'s head into the breeze.
Positioned thus, no guns could come to bear,
advantage that *Linnet* was quick to seize.

Exposed, the captain dropped behind the line
to make repairs and hastily return.
When he restored ability to fight
he stationed *Eagle* off the flagship's stern.

The movements *Eagle* made caused great concern
aboard the flagship, now in danger's way.
Linnet and *Confiance* could double up
on *Saratoga* – thus to win the day.

Macdonough's preparation and his skill
now took the battle on its final course.
His starboard guns disabled he began
a tactic that remade his ship a force.

He sent below his gun crews that remained
and used kedge anchors, hausers, and a winch
to turn ship where he anchored long before
he met *Chubb, Confiance, Linnet,* and *Finch.*

Linnet increased its fire to stop the turn
while *Confiance* tried copying the move.
The British ship was not equipped to match
maneuvers that Macdonough was to prove.

Since *Eagle* took its new place in the line
it concentrated fire on *Confiance*.
But *Saratoga* drew the British fire,
and *Eagle* had quite limited response.

With Tom Macdonough's turn at last complete,
he called his gunners to the larboard side.
These unused and undamaged guns were now
prepared to keep the British occupied.

The first two broadsides had severe effects;
the crew of *Confiance* could fight no more.
Reluctantly, the captain gave command
to strike the flag; an act he would deplore.

Macdonough knew the battle wasn't done
but now his ship's head once again must change.
Continuing his turning move, he brought
Linnet within his larboard broadside range.

Uneven though the contest had become,
the valiant crew fought for a quarter hour.
About to sink, *Linnet* at last gave up.
Americans retained Lake Champlain power.

In Plattsburgh, the invading British troops
would quickly learn about the lake defeat.
Commanding General Prevost feared supply
lines would be cut; he ordered a retreat.

The battle lasted two and one half hours,
but its impact would last for many years.
Invading forces were sent home for good
by brave intrepid Navy volunteers.

   * * * * * * *

When *Confiance* finally struck colors, it had sustained 105 holes in its hull; *Saratoga* had 55. Captain Daniel Pring, the senior remaining British officer, assembled his commanders on *Saratoga*'s deck to present their swords to the victorious American. Macdonough responded: "Gentlemen, your gallant conduct makes you worthy to wear your weapons; return them to their scabbards." Macdonough then dispatched the following message to Secretary of the Navy William Jones: "Sir: The Almighty has been pleased to grant us a signal victory on Lake Champlain, in the capture of one frigate, one brig, and two sloops of war, of the enemy." The London Times reported: "This is a lamentable event to the civilized world." The Battle of Lake Champlain and the resulting ending of British invasion plans removed all leverage the British had at the peace council at Ghent. The Peace Treaty was signed on Christmas Eve, 1814, ceding Great Britain none of the territory it sought.

Thomas Macdonough was honored by Congress with promotion to captain. He served as Commandant, Portsmouth Navy Yard from 1815 to 1818, then commanded *Guerriere* in the Mediterranean. He later commanded *Constitution* in the Mediterranean but was relieved because of poor health. He died at sea on November 10, 1825, en route home.

12. The End of Barbary Piracy

Appropriately, the adventures recounted in this book that featured Stephen Decatur in three earlier episodes, will end with the retelling of his final important accomplishment. While the United States was engaged in war with England, the Barbary states broke their peace treaties. Shortly after the peace treaty with England was ratified, President Madison took decisive action.

The End of Barbary Piracy

While the United States was fully involved in the war with Great Britain, Algiers and the other Barbary States decided to break their peace treaty with the United States and resume pirating merchantmen and enslaving their crews. This enraged President Madison and, as soon as the peace treaty with Great Britain was ratified in 1815, he decided to send a large squadron of ships to the Mediterranean to deal with the problem. The first group of ten ships would leave from New York as soon as they could be fitted out. The second would leave from Boston a couple of months later. Stephen Decatur accepted command of the first group with *Guerriere* his flagship, with the understanding that when the second group arrived under the command of William Bainbridge (Decatur's senior officer), Decatur's group would join the second group, all would be under Bainbridge's command, and Decatur would be free to sail back to the United States.

   *   *   *   *   *   *   *

Decatur wished to get his squadron set
to leave New York as soon as they were fit.
He had a reputation to uphold;
he saw to fitting out from stern to sprit.

By 20 May he was prepared to start,
parading his impressive fleet to sea.
His flagship *Guerriere* was first in line,
its crew decked out to show its high esprit.

Decatur planned to end the pirates' reign
before the later squadron could arrive.
His plans required some action early on
to justify the bargain he would drive.

With him was William Shaler, diplomat,
to help with treaties, if his plans worked out.
The ocean crossing went without event;
in Tangier he learned much to excise doubt

that he would be in action very soon.
Reis Hammida, the well-known Algerine,
an admiral of great repute, just two
days earlier, in Tangier, had been seen.

Decatur reached Gibralter June 15
and learned Hammida was off Cape de Gatte,
awaiting Spanish tribute payment there.
Decatur headed quickly toward the spot

he hoped he would locate his enemy.
The second day, while off the Spanish shore,
Decatur's lookouts saw a sail ahead;
he headed east in order to explore.

When full sails blossomed from the unknown ship,
Decatur sensed he'd found the foe he sought.
Mashouda was the ship that tried to flee,
but in a while, the Algerine was caught.

As *Guerriere* closed in for the attack,
Mashouda fired – the battle had begun.
For twenty minutes fighting was intense,
until *Mashouda* signaled it was done.

Decatur sent a prize crew to assess
the damage and the situation there.
They learned the feared, Reis Hammida, was dead;
the damage to the ship they could repair.

12-1. USS Guerriere vs. Mashouda

Decatur had the prize crew take the ship
and prisoners to Cartagena, Spain,
awaiting further orders. Then, the hunt
for other Algerines began again.

Within two days a brig was spotted close
to shore – an Algerine; the chase began.
The ship, *Estedio*, soon ran aground,
a helpless prey for the American.

A second prize crew took the brig and crew
to Cartagena. Now he had in hand
two ships, almost five hundred prisoners:
the chips to bargain with, as he had planned.

Just thirty days since he had left New York,
Decatur took his squadron to Algiers.
The ten great ships with colors high were now
the largest fleet of warships seen in years.

A white flag flew from *Guerriere*'s mast head,
and Sweden's flag was hoisted – thus to mean
Decatur wished negotiations now
with Sweden's consul as a go-between.

Around midday, a boat approached from town
with Swedish consul and port captain there.
Aboard the ship, the men went right to work;
Decatur led by making them aware

that he had captured two Algerine ships,
and Admiral Hammida had been killed.
The captain of the port appeared in shock;
the atmosphere Decatur wished to build.

The captain said that meetings should take place
on land. Decatur answered that the site
for future talks would be aboard his ship;
his tone was always firm, but still polite.

12-2. Decatur's Fleet at Algiers

The captain and the consul left the ship,
and met the dey that night. Both men returned
next day with the authority to move
the process on; the captain was concerned

that the Americans had all the strength
to press their plans. Decatur did just that.
He handed them a treaty draft that he
had drawn up with his onboard diplomat.

Provisions called for universal peace,
most favored nation status for their trade,
cessation of all payments of tribute,
a prisoner exchange, and no blockade.

The tribute payment clause would cause some pain,
but when Decatur gave his word the ships
that he had captured would be given back –
the end to war seemed at their fingertips.

The dey approved the treaty; Shaler moved
ashore as consul general that day.
Sardinia would be the fleet's next stop
for rest and fresh supplies: a ten-day stay.

Decatur moved with haste to Tunis next
to show the bey the treaty he achieved.
The dey of Algiers pact and threat of force
brought more success; Decatur then received

a treaty from the bey of Tunis, signed,
and with the strong conditions like the first.
In Tripoli, the bashaw never thought
this warrior would, in peace work, be immersed.

However, he too yielded to the strength
and gave Decatur just what he had sought.
In less than eighty days he stopped a war,
and only minor battles had been fought.

When he met Bainbridge, who had just arrived, he changed command as previously planned. In *Guerriere* he sailed back to New York with three war-ending treaties in his hand.

* * * * * * *

Of the many achievements of his illustrious Naval career, Stephen Decatur considered this his most significant. The troubles with the Barbary states had continued for years with many United States' merchantmen having been captured and the crews enslaved. When the Treaty of Ghent was ratified, and President Madison decided the piracy must end, he dispatched Stephen Decatur, who brought the Barbary states to heel in less time than anyone thought possible.

* * * * * * *

Commodore James Barron, commanding the frigate **USS Chesapeake**, took his ship to sea with an inexperienced crew on June 22, 1807. The ship was confronted by **HMS Leopold**, demanding to search **Chesapeake** for British deserters. Barron refused, and **Leopold** attacked. Outgunned, Barron surrendered after firing just one gun. Barron was court-martialed, and Stephen Decatur was ordered to sit on the court. The court found Barron guilty and suspended him from the Navy for five years. Barron always blamed Decatur for his humiliation, and years later he challenged Decatur to a dual. On March 22, 1820 the men faced each other in a field at Bladensburg, Maryland. Barron suffered a serious hip injury, but Decatur was mortally wounded. He died later that day at age 41, a tragic end to an illustrious career. His funeral was attended by the President, the Supreme Court, many members of Congress, and about 10,000 citizens paid respects to their national hero. He was interred in St. Peter's Church in Philadelphia.

Epilogue

The extraordinary *sailors* featured in this book shared many admirable characteristics that led to their being placed in situations that tested them to the full. Their accomplishments speak volumes on how well they measured up to their most difficult assignments and experiences. What was it about James Lawrence that motivated the surviving members of his crew, when their captain and many fellow crewmen were dying or dead, to refuse to lower the flag? Why did they face almost certain death rather than ignore his final exhortation: "Don't give up the ship; fight her till she sinks!" It's called **leadership**.

The Leader is ...

the one they look to when they've lost their way;
the one who raises spirits when they're down;
the one who will go back to help a stray;
the one who leads, but never wears a crown;

the one who will endure the daily pain;
the one who will provide the needed spark;
the one who works for good, and not for gain;
the one who finds the light amid the dark;

the one who stands apart, though in a crowd;
the one who will solve problems that arise;
the one who always speaks the truth aloud;
the one who will support, not criticize;

the one who listens to another's view;
the one who lives with energy and verve;
the one who will commit and follow through.
The leader is the one who's called to serve.

Edward W. Lull

The Author

Edward Lull is an Executive Director of The Poetry Society of Virginia, having served four one-year terms as its president. In his first career, he was a naval officer serving primarily in submarines. He shaped a second career in business with small, hi-tech firms in the Washington, D.C. area. Lull has a bachelors degree from the United States Naval Academy and a masters from The George Washington University. He published his first book, a historical novel written in blank verse, entitled: *Cabin Boy to Captain: a Sea Story,* in 2003. The second, an anthology of his poems, entitled *Where Giants Walked*, was published in 2005. Earlier Lull edited an anthology of poems for the Williamsburg Poetry Guild, entitled *Vintage Wine and Good Spirits.* In 2006, he co-edited a book, *Four Virginia Poets Laureate: A Teaching Guide,* with the current Poet Laureate of Virginia, Carolyn Kreiter-Foronda. He has won awards for his poetry from Florida State Poets Association, West Virginia Poetry Society, Chicagoland Poetry Contest, Poets at Work, as well as several from The Poetry Society of Virginia. Lull and his wife Evelyn live in Williamsburg, Virginia. They have three children and eight grandchildren.